Jane Austen
and Lyme Regis

Lyme from the Church Cliffs.

Jane Austen and Lyme Regis

MAGGIE LANE

THE JANE AUSTEN SOCIETY

First published in Great Britain 2003
by the Jane Austen Society
c/o Jane Austen's House, Chawton, Hampshire GU34 1SD
© Copyright 2003 Maggie Lane

ISBN 9538174-2-3

Printed by Sarsen Press, Hyde Street, Winchester

For Tabitha

Contents

Acknowledgements

This book was written at the behest of the Jane Austen Society to fill a real gap, the only other book on the subject being R.A. Austen-Leigh's 1941 *Jane Austen and Lyme Regis*, now a collector's item. I would like to thank fellow members of the Jane Austen Society Executive Committee Deirdre Le Faye, Helen Lefroy, David Selwyn, Diana Shervington and Brian Southam for their advice and help, with the usual disclaimer that any errors remain my own.

Staff in both the Philpot Museum and Lyme Regis Library were very helpful in answering my queries. I am specially grateful to the Philpot Museum for permission to use the illustrations on p.20 and 40. Society member and graphic designer Jane Odiwe most kindly created the map on pp. 26-27. Nigel Cozens of Lymelight Books and Prints helped me choose old prints of Lyme. The illustration from *Persuasion* on p.30 is reproduced by kind permission of the Folio Society. My ever-helpful friend Diana Birchall allowed me to use her photograph on page 5. My thanks are also due to the descendants of Jane Austen's brother Francis for permission to use Cassandra Austen's watercolour on the back of this book.

The Jane Austen Society gratefully acknowledges financial support in the production of this book from Lyme Regis Town Council.

THE HARBOUR, LYME REGIS.

Introduction

Lyme Regis, a small town on the Dorset coast, shares with the city of
Bath the distinction of appearing in the work of Jane Austen, and of
being often visited by her admirers on that account. In both places it is
possible, with a little guidance and a little imagination, to walk in her
characters' footsteps and to see something of what they saw nearly two
hundred years ago. For the modern visitor to Lyme, sauntering on the
Cobb, exploring the narrow streets of the old town, and enjoying the
natural beauty of the cliffs and shore, it is easy to see how the place
captured her imagination.

For whereas she was at best ambivalent about Bath, Jane Austen felt
great affection for Lyme, as is clear from the heartfelt passages of
description which usher in the seaside scenes in *Persuasion*. Only two
chapters of that novel are set in Lyme, yet they are two of the most
memorable chapters in the whole body of her work, in terms both of
action and of feeling.

It happens that both the only letter and the only picture we have of
Jane Austen from her late twenties are associated with Lyme. In these

years the Austen family, from their base in Bath, visited several of the seaside resorts then springing up along the south coast of England. The letter that Jane Austen wrote from Lyme in September 1804 is the only one to survive between May 1801 (when she had just moved to Bath) and January 1805 (when her father died), and is therefore the only letter from a distinct period of her life, a period in which she uniquely travelled for exploration and pleasure. Though the information it gives is relatively scanty – she was not writing for the benefit of scholars – the letter shows her at twenty-eight years old, walking, bathing, dancing and observing the company: a young woman on holiday in an early nineteenth-century resort.

The painting shown on the back cover of this book is dated 1804 and according to a niece, was done by her sister Cassandra, on one of their "expeditions", hence almost certainly in the countryside around Lyme.

Lyme Regis was the only resort to which the Austens returned a second year, suggesting that they agreed with the narrator of *Persuasion* that "a very strange stranger it must be who does not see charms in the immediate environs of Lyme, to make him wish to know it better," and that "these places must be visited, and visited again, to make the worth of Lyme understood". No other place in England receives quite such an endorsement from Jane Austen.

For all these reasons, a fresh look at Lyme in the life and work of Jane Austen is overdue. This little book aims to give a full account of what is known of Jane Austen's visits to Lyme and the surrounding area; to explore her use of the town in *Persuasion;* to disentangle the various attempts at identifying locations that have been made over the years, and provide a guide to what may still be seen of Jane Austen's Lyme.

To put her experiences there in context, it is necessary to begin with an episode in the Austen family history, and to describe something of the early history of Lyme itself and the rise of the seaside resort in the years immediately preceding Jane Austen's visits.

"Future Summers by the Sea":
the Austens in the West Country

For the first twenty-five years of her life Jane Austen lived at Steventon Rectory in Hampshire. Born in December 1775, she was the seventh of the eight children of the Rector. With her only sister, Cassandra, she spent two brief periods at boarding school, and the family often paid long visits to relations, chiefly in Kent. But her imaginative life was founded on the security of home. She had already written three novels at Steventon, though she had been unsuccessful in getting anything published.

Towards the end of 1800 her parents made what appears to have been a sudden decision to leave the parish to the care of their eldest son and to settle, with their two unmarried daughters, in Bath. For Mr and Mrs Austen, this was a well-deserved retirement in a place they found congenial and cheerful. For their daughters, both in their mid-twenties, it was an unwelcome uprooting from a beloved home. The news came as a total shock to Jane and she had to struggle to reconcile herself to it. Many years later she seems to have given her own feelings to Anne Elliot, the twenty-seven-year-old heroine of *Persuasion,* who "disliked Bath, and did not think it agreed with her" and who, forced to make it her home, "persisted in a very determined, though very silent, disinclination for Bath".

Anne Elliot particularly dreads "the possible heats of September in all the white glare of Bath". This, at least, Jane Austen herself would be spared. Part of her parents' plan was that they would escape the stifling atmosphere and bad smells of the city each year by taking extended holidays on the coast.

"The prospect of spending future summers by the Sea or in Wales is very delightful,"[1] wrote Jane in a letter to Cassandra, trying to make the best of the change that was being forced on them. There is no firm evidence that the family ever ventured into Wales, but for the next few years they took lodgings for several weeks in one of the newly-fashionable West Country resorts.

And unwelcome though the change may have been at the time, there is no doubt that her experience both of Bath and of the seaside enlarged Jane Austen's knowledge of her society and provided abundant material for transmuting, years later, into fiction.

Jane Austen in Devon

A hankering for the sea in fact slightly pre-dated the Austens' decision to move to Bath, suggesting that the seaside part of their plan was no mere afterthought. In November 1800, before Bath had been mentioned, Jane wrote to Cassandra that she had had a most affectionate letter from Richard Buller, a man of about her own age who had been a boarding pupil in Steventon Rectory, now married and appointed Vicar of Colyton, in East Devon. "He is very pressing in his invitation to us all to come & see him at Colyton, & my father is very much inclined to go there next Summer. – It is a circumstance that may considerably assist the Dawlish scheme," wrote Jane.[2]

The fame of Dawlish was such that in *Sense and Sensibility* Jane Austen could poke fun at Robert Ferrars' ignorance by stating, "It seemed rather surprising to him that anybody could live in Devonshire, without living in Dawlish". However, the less geographically challenged Austens quickly realised that it would make sense to combine the visit to Colyton with a stay not in Dawlish but in Sidmouth, on the same side of the Exe estuary. "Sidmouth is now talked of as our summer abode," reported Jane in January 1801.[3]

Accordingly, having spent some time house-hunting in Bath, and having signed a three-year lease, they left the city for a while. We have corroborative evidence in a letter from Jane's cousin Eliza, now married to Henry Austen, dated 29 October 1801. "I conclude you know of our Uncle & Aunt Austen and their daughters having spent the summer in Devonshire," she wrote to a mutual cousin. "They are now returned to Bath where they are superintending the fitting up of their new house. Their eldest Son James is now in possession of Steventon...."[4]. We know no more of this, their first seaside tour – it was only when Jane

Colyton Rectory (photo: Diana Birchall)

5

and Cassandra were separated that letters between them, which give us such vital information, could exist. But it seems reasonable to suppose that they did visit Richard and Anna Buller in their lovely Tudor Vicarage in the historic inland town of Colyton, and that the rest of their holiday was spent at Sidmouth.

The following year the Austens achieved their ambition of staying in Dawlish. Although again, no letters from this period exist, our authority for the 1802 holiday comes from a reference Jane Austen made in 1814, when she wrote of Dawlish to a niece that "the Library was particularly pitiful & wretched 12 years ago"[5].

There is a tradition, put about by later generations of the family, that during one of these holidays in Devon Jane Austen fell in love with a young man who returned her feelings, but that he died before they could meet again. Her niece Caroline is the earliest written source of the story, having heard it from her Aunt Cassandra in her old age. Caroline did not write anything down until she was old herself, and then she says that she was sure it was in Devonshire and not in Lyme that the romance happened – she would have remembered if Cassandra had said Lyme.

For it was in Lyme that Jane Austen spent the next two summers, those of 1803 an 1804. Her delight in the place was to inspire a passage in *Persuasion,* that tender yet mature love story that is redolent both of season and of landscape. This is why, if told that her aunt's own "love story" had taken place in Lyme, Caroline would have registered the significance. But Jane Austen was both too thorough an artist, and too private a person, to work so blatantly from life.

Lyme before Jane Austen

The name Lyme Bay refers not just to the little bay in which the town itself nestles, but to a sixty-mile sweep of coastline from Portland in Dorset to Start Point in Devon. It is evidence of Lyme's ancient importance that, despite being so small and inaccessible itself, it should have given its name to such a large part of the southern English coast.

Lyme or Lyme Regis?
The fact that Jane Austen never uses the word 'Regis', even in writing for publication, may have led some readers to suppose that it was a later suffix, perhaps something to do with the Prince Regent. Nothing could be farther from the truth. Lyme Regis (meaning King's Lyme) dates from 1284, when Edward I gave it a royal charter. This was not an especial honour – it was one of eight granted in the same year – but a strategy to make money for the crown. In return for certain trading privileges and their own minor courts, these towns had to pay an annual rent and taxes to the royal exchequer, administered and collected by the King's Bailiff. Lyme was also entitled to send two members to Parliament, a practice that became increasingly hard to justify as the town shrank in national significance but which endured right up to the great Reform Act of 1832.[6]

The Cobb Lyme Regis.

So why does Jane Austen never use the full name? My theory is that in her experience people talked just about 'Lyme', and that it was only with a later growth in civic pride across the country that 'Regis' came into common use again. The novelist and diarist Fanny Burney, writing in the 1790s, also omits the word 'Regis' (though spelling the town 'Lime').

The Cobb

From medieval times, therefore, Lyme was a considerable trading port, exporting mainly wool and importing wine and other Mediterranean commodities. It also built ships. As proof of its maritime activity, in 1347 at the siege of Calais, Lyme was able to provide four ships, as against Portsmouth's five, and 62 mariners. In 1677 it was the fourteenth largest port in the whole of England. Yet in topographical terms, Lyme was an unlikely place to site a port.

There was no natural harbour: that was remedied early in its history by building the Cobb, which acts not only as shelter for ships but as a giant breakwater, protecting the land from buffeting by the sea, coming in on the prevailing westerly winds. Then, the land itself is notoriously unstable, frequently slipping into the sea and preventing the spread of building along the cliffs. Thirdly, and most amazingly, the steepness of the hinterland meant that until as late as 1759, no wheeled traffic could get into Lyme. From the old Roman inland east-west road (the present A35), only tracks led steeply down to the town. All the goods for export and import, everything required to sustain the town, if it did not come round by sea, came and went by packhorse. Residents and visitors (very few of *them)* had the choice of horseback or their own two feet. No coaches, no wagons, until within fifty years of Jane Austen's visit.

Labouring under so many difficulties imposed by nature, Lyme owes almost everything to the man-made wonders of the Cobb. For five hundred years it made Lyme's existence as a town economically viable. Increasingly since 1818, as the scene of the most dramatic moment in one of the best-loved novels in the English language, its fame has spread all over the world. (And in our own times, resident novelist John Fowles, setting *The French Lieutenant's Woman* in Lyme, and abetted by the film and its poster showing Meryl Streep in a cloak on the end of the Cobb, has brought this structure yet more literary fame.) For thousands of people, even those who have never seen it, the Cobb is part of their mental scenery.

The Cobb is first mentioned in documents in 1295, though some date before 1250 is estimated for its construction. There has never been any wholly satisfactory explanation for its name, but it may be related to the word cobblestone. For centuries, it was not the solid structure known to Jane Austen and ourselves, but large boulders crammed between walls of oak trunks. A drawing of 1539 shows these wooden piles quite clearly. No mortar was used to hold the stones in place. Repairs and renewal had constantly to be undertaken. A beach a few miles west of Lyme supplied the boulders, which were floated between barrels to where they were wanted. In 1545, 61 tree trunks had to be brought from eight miles away, the nearer ones presumably having been used up (on ship- and house-building, as well as the Cobb).

The Cobb was one of the wonders of medieval and Tudor engineering, and was unique. The men of Lyme who could construct and maintain such an edifice in marine conditions were held in high regard. This method of construction lasted until the eighteenth century. The other difference between the Cobb of old and now is that, as early prints of Lyme show, at high tide it did not link wholly to the land. This allowed great quantities of shingle to sweep in from the west and be deposited like an apron in front of the town, giving further protection from sea erosion. The gap was not closed until 1756.

Lyme and the Stuarts

Against this background of constant battle with the forces of nature to hold on to its share of England's prosperity, Lyme featured twice in the more stirring events of history. During the Civil War, it was on the side of Parliament, and was besieged by the Royalists under the command of Prince Maurice, brother of the more famous Prince Rupert. As they heavily outnumbered the Parliamentary forces in the town – 6,000 men on the Royalist side, 4,000 townsfolk and a garrison of 600 – they expected an easy victory. But, with the help of supplies from the sea, the town withstood a two-month siege, until the Royalists gave up and marched away. It is recorded that the women in the town helped dig trenches and load muskets, their traditional red shawls giving the impression from the hills that there were more fighting men in the town than really were.

Forty-one years later the Duke of Monmouth, Charles II's illegitimate son, chose Lyme from which to launch his attack on the throne of his Catholic uncle, James II. In choosing Lyme, Monmouth gambled on support from the traditionally Puritan stronghold. With a force of some eighty men, he appeared out of the blue on June 11th 1685, having sailed in three small ships from Amsterdam. He landed on the beach west of the Cobb now known as Monmouth beach and spent three days recruiting in the town. He then set off on his march north, gathering men as he went, until reaching the outskirts of Bristol, which he dared not attack. Looping back, he was met by the King's forces and defeated at the Battle of Sedgemoor in Somerset on July 6th. He was taken to the Tower of London, granted an audience with James II in which he begged for mercy, but was hanged on July 15th.

In September, punishment was meted out to Lyme when, as part of his retributive progress round the West Country, Judge Jeffreys arrived to sentence twelve men to death by hanging, all but one of them to quartering too. One man escaped the latter fate because the Judge accepted a bribe of £1000 from his sister. The grisly tarred remains of the eleven were hung about the town as an example and were, apparently, only cleared away after 1688, when William of Orange made a more propitious landing at Brixham in Devon and the unlamented James II was finally dislodged.

The Royal connection was more pleasantly renewed in 1727 when the wedding dress of Queen Caroline, wife of George II, was fashioned from lace made by the women of Lyme. But already Lyme's prosperity was declining. The woollen industry was moving north, repeated wars with France were discouraging the wine trade, and in any case the Cobb was not large enough for the bigger ships of the day. After decades of stagnation, in which the population declined and many houses were left abandoned and falling down, Lyme was saved by the growth of a completely different commercial activity in which it claimed its share: travel by the upper and middle classes for novelty and pleasure. This was the movement which would bring Jane Austen and Lyme together and give Lyme a kind of immortality it could not have dreamed of during all those centuries as a hard-working port.

The Rise of the Seaside Resort

The seaside had always been there, so why did visiting the coast for health and amusement arise when it did, in the second half of the eighteenth century? As is usually the case with any cultural new direction, several factors combined. Big improvements in both roads and carriages made travel for pleasure feasible, not just something to be endured. Nature, so long man's adversary, was being tamed, and could thus be encountered from choice. Long wars with France meant that Continental travel was often impossible: the rich had to be restless at home. William Gilpin, with his writings on the Picturesque, and then the Romantic poets, opened people's eyes to the beauty of natural scenery and the thrill of journeying into the more inaccessible areas of the British Isles.

The inland spas such as Bath had innovated and established the vogue for holidays, with all their attendant rituals and activities, but had suffered from their own success, becoming too populous, tame and built-up to suit the modern taste. People whose parents and grandparents had marvelled over the clean pavements, good shops and highly organised assemblies of Bath were now beginning to seek out wildness, grandeur and emptiness. By definition, the coast offered these things to a greater or lesser degree. Hitherto, only those who made their living from the sea had dreamt of living in its vicinity. (And *they* usually turned their back on the sea, or built a little way inland.) It only took somebody – in fact a clever Dr Russell – to decide that sea water was just as efficacious as spa water, either for drinking or immersion, for a whole new industry to start up.

As with the inland spas, the quest for health led the way, but the desire for novelty to while away abundant leisure played no small part. Whereas at the beginning of the eighteenth century Bath had sufficed for the small proportion of the population who could afford to leave home, by the end that proportion was much bigger and their spending power could support a more widespread tourist industry.

Eighteenth-century sea-bathing
Dr Russell's medical treatise in favour of sea-bathing began the process by turning the little fishing village of Brighthelmstone in Sussex into the fashionable watering-place Brighton, patronised from the 1780s by the Prince of Wales and his pleasure-loving friends. But just as the Prince and his father King George III each openly favoured a different political party, so each had his favourite seaside resort in which he held court and set the pattern of activity. George III first visited Weymouth, Lyme's Dorset neighbour, in 1789 to recuperate from the first frightening attack of his illness, believed now to be porphyria but then ascribed to madness. The place agreed with him, and he made visits there a regular fixture of his year. His days, too, were paid out with monotonous regularity, from his 5am rise, his early bathe, his 3pm dinner and his 6pm promenade on the Esplanade. Between 1798 and 1805 he and members of his large family paid fourteen summer or autumn visits to Weymouth.

Now both the raffish and the respectable elements of society had their role models in the practice of sea-visiting and sea-bathing. Everyone who could afford it could find justification for indulging in this new pleasure. "And all, impatient of dry land, agree / With one consent to rush into the sea," as Jane Austen's favourite poet, William Cowper, wrote.

In the early years, sea-bathing was considered particularly efficacious if undertaken in cold weather and early in the morning, when the pores were supposed to be closed. "To Bathe late in the Day (more especially in hot Weather) will occasion great depression of Spirits," wrote Dr Crane of Weymouth[7]. Guided by the medical profession, the first seaside holidays were often taken at unseasonable times of the year. In an early journal Fanny Burney described such a visit to Brighton in

The caption to this Cruikshank print reads: "Hydromania – or a touch of the sub-Lyme and Beautiful. The Beach at Lyme Regis.

14

November 1782: "We rose at six o'clock in the morn and by the pale blink o' the moon went to the seaside where we had bespoken the bathing-woman to be ready for us, and into the ocean we plunged. It was cold but pleasant. I have bathed so often as to lose my dread of the operation."

Even more horrific was the case of Jane Austen's own cousin, the widowed Eliza de Feuillide, who spent January and February 1791 at Margate in Kent for the sake of her sickly little son. A doctor had assured her that "one months [sic] bathing at this time of year was

From an original sketch by an amateur 8 September 1819." It is thought the nudity was imaginary!

more efficacious than Six at any other…. The Sea has strengthened him wonderfully & I think has likewise been of great service to myself, I still continue bathing notwithstanding the severity of the Weather and Frost and Snow, which I think somewhat courageous."[8]

Eighteenth-century bathers did not wade or leap into the sea and splash or swim at will. They entered a wheeled bathing-machine on the beach, which was then pulled out by horse or manpower to a reasonable depth. One or two burly women attendants then guided or pushed the bather into the sea; with no chance to acclimatise to the temperature of the water, this must often have been a shock to the system. The bather would be held under from the shoulders for a specified period of immersion. Women wore shifts, men were naked from the waist up. A satirical print of 1818 entitled 'Hydromania' shows women bathing naked at Lyme, observed by a man with a telescope, but this is certainly an exaggeration of the truth.

The medical profession certainly liked to dictate how things should be done. Although Dr Russell assured his readers that "sea water is embued with many and great virtues," he advised "the unskilful may make very bad use". Such cautions influenced even such an experienced bather as Fanny Burney. At Sidmouth in 1791, in the favourable month of August, she found "the sea was as calm & gentle as the Thames. I longed to Bathe, but I am in no state now to take liberties with myself, &, having no advice at hand, I ran no risk."[9]

The development of Lyme
"Since George III introduced the fashion of regularly going to the southern coast for health, doctors have been advising it in all consumptive cases," wrote a Dr Granville. "The particular spot designated for this purpose has extended west and south, farther and farther every eight or ten years; from Weymouth to Sidmouth, from Sidmouth to Exmouth, and so on to Dawlish and Teignmouth."

It is notable that Lyme, historically a much more considerable place than Dawlish, is not mentioned in this litany, but it was certainly part of the scramble to be developed, even before George III's endorsement of Weymouth. It is thought that the first visits for pleasure happened in the 1750s, but certainly by the 1770s, under pressure from one individual, the town was beginning to take itself seriously as a resort.

That individual was Thomas Hollis (1720-1774). It is perhaps no more than co-incidence that Hollis should be the surname of the first husband of Lady Denham, and the source of her wealth, in the fragment written by Jane Austen in the last months before her death in 1817. *Sanditon*, as the fragment is known, is all about the development of an unremarkable little fishing village into a would-be fashionable seaside resort in competition with its neighbours. The moving spirits are the two resident landholders, Thomas Parker, who seems to act out of an excess of energy and exaggerated partiality for his native place, and Lady Denham, whose motive is pure avarice.

The motives of the real Thomas Hollis are harder to fathom at this distance. He was a man of fervent republican and radical views, a benefactor of Harvard University in the United States of America. He retired to his estate at Corscombe, near Beaminster, just a few miles from Lyme, but he also kept permanent rooms in the Three Cups hotel at the bottom of Broad Street, dubbing them 'Liberty Hall'. He bought up much of the semi-derelict property in the town in order to demolish it and improve the views. He purchased land by the shore to create the first public promenade, 'The Walk' as it would have been known to Jane Austen (now part of Marine Parade). And he knocked down warehouses to clear a site for the Assembly Rooms, completed just after his death in 1775 – the year of Jane Austen's birth.

If Weymouth had its King and Brighton its Prince, thanks to Thomas Hollis Lyme soon had its Prime Minister in the person of the Earl of Chatham, who at the suggestion of his friend Hollis brought his sickly son to Lyme in 1772. Chatham liked Lyme so much he wanted to buy the house they stayed in – now marked with a plaque – but the owners would not sell. The place evidently did the boy good (as did Hollis's political and philosophical conversations) since he grew up to be an even greater Prime Minister than his father, and known to us as William Pitt the Younger, the longest-serving and most important Prime Minister of Jane Austen's lifetime.

Hollis, and his counterparts elsewhere, including in *Sanditon*, well understood that though the paying public now wanted something wilder than Bath, or even Brighton, they still expected certain amenities in the new coastal resorts. Newly-built lodgings, Assembly Rooms, shops, libraries and dry places to promenade were created to fulfil the holiday-makers' needs and relieve them of their money. But Lyme, for all the natural beauty of its surroundings, still suffered from the same geographical disadvantages that had held it back before. The instability of the land to both sides of the River Lym meant the town continued to be crammed into the narrow valley. Though with time detached villas began to appear on the slopes behind the town, there was no scope for the elegant terraces and crescents that other places were building at the sea-shore itself. This is perhaps what Jane Austen means when she says in *Persuasion* "there is nothing to admire in the buildings themselves" before going on to praise the scenery.

Fanny Burney and Lyme

A letter from Fanny Burney twelve years before Jane Austen's visit is worth quoting as it vividly illustrates the contemporary response to Lyme – the hinterland so well calculated to appeal to the imagination of the period, and the town itself so liable to disappoint. Burney was making an extended tour of the South of England following her release from five years' immurement at the Court of George III, where she had held the position of Mistress of the Wardrobe to Queen Charlotte. She writes in the language of one, like Jane Austen, conversant with the Picturesque, yet without Jane Austen's usual ironical approach. Though she was 39, and self-confessedly in low spirits, she describes with all the ardour of a Marianne Dashwood:

Monday, Augst 8 [1791]. We proceeded to Bridport, a remarkably clean Town, with the air so clear & pure, it seemed a new climate. Hence we set out, after Dinner, for Lime [*sic*], & the Road through which we travelled is the most beautiful to which my wandering destinies have yet sent me. It is diversified with all that can compose luxuriant scenery, & with just as much of the approach to the sublime, as is in the province of unterrific beauty. The Hills are the highest, I fancy, in the South of this country, the boldest, & noblest; - the vales of the finest verdure, wooded & watered as if only to give ideas of finished Landscapes; while the whole, from time to time, rises into still superior grandeur, by openings between the heights that terminate the view with the splendour of the British Channel. There was no going on in the carriage through such enchanting scenes; We got out upon the Hills, & walked till we could walk no longer.

The descent down to Lime is uncommonly steep; & indeed it is very striking, from the magnificence of the Ocean that washes its borders. Chideock, & Charmouth, two villages between Bridport & Lime, are the very prettiest I have ever seen.

During the whole of this Post [*i.e. stage* of their journey], I was fairly taken away, not only from the World, but from myself, & completely wrapped up & engrossed by the pleasures – wonders - & charms of animating Nature, thus seen in fair perfection.

Lime, however, brought me to myself; for the part by the Sea, where we fixt our abode was so dirty, & *fishy,* that I rejoiced when we left it.[10] She went on to Sidmouth which she found "more pleasant & more commodious" and where, as we have seen, she longed to bathe.

Lyme in the 1800s

When the first national census was taken in 1801, two years before Jane Austen's first visit to Lyme, the town had a population of 1,400; by 1811 it had risen to 1,925. In 1806 it was visited by Harriette Wilson,

The Assembly Rooms, Lyme Regis by Mr. Read, 1815
(Courtesy of the Philpot Museum)

the courtesan, as a very young woman. In her *Memoirs* written in 1825 she recalled, "Lyme Regis is a sort of Brighton in miniature, all bustle and confusion, assembly-rooms, donkey-riding, raffling etc. etc. The society was chiefly composed of people of very small independent fortunes, who for economy, had settled at Lyme Regis; or of such who required sea bathing."

The Assembly Rooms were the chief boast of the place, and were said to be modelled on those at Bath. They were, however, built on a very cramped site at Cobb Gate, the foot of Broad Street, and pressed right against the sea. Besides several ante-rooms and offices, there was a card room, with billiard-room above it, and a double-height rectangular ballroom, the long wall of which was pierced by a row of sash windows overlooking the sea, while the end wall consisted almost entirely of a large bay window facing across the sands to the Cobb. The orchestra comprised three violins and a violoncello, and three glass chandeliers lit up the room by night. London and provincial papers were available for reading, tea and coffee were served at one shilling per person, and sedan chairs were kept "for the accommodation of the Company".

The other fashionable accoutrements of the place were the bathing machines – four in Jane Austen's day – and the beginning of a promenade around the bay, known as 'The Walk'. Only one year after the Austens' second visit, the amenities were increased by an indoor baths, known as Jefford's, where the present Marine Theatre stands.

We can catch the flavour of the place much as Jane Austen would have known it from the *Guide to All the Watering and Sea-Bathing Places*, published anonymously in 1810, just six years after her second visit. The general tone of the guide is laudatory, as it seeks to recommend the various resorts to new visitors. In speaking of Lyme, however, its tone can be caustic:

Lyme is built on the declivity of a craggy hill, at the head of an inlet of the sea, and contains many respectable looking houses, with pleasant gardens, particularly in the upper part of the town; but the streets are steep, rugged and unpleasant. In the lower part the houses are mean, and the streets so intricate, that a stranger, it has been wittily remarked, will sometimes find himself bewildered, as if he were entangled in a forest, or the labyrinth of a fox-den. Here the lower order of the inhabitants in general reside, having that position which nature and fortune assigned to them. To be a person of consideration in Lyme, it is necessary to toil up hill, and to fix one's abode where it is in danger of being assailed by every wind that blows.

Although we cannot be certain where the Austens lodged in either 1803 or 1804, as we shall see, the indications are that on both dates they were in the lower part of the town, hence with the lower orders! Captain Harville, too, is most decidedly given "a residence unexpensive, and by the sea" – at sea level, indeed.

The *Guide* continues:

Altogether, however, Lyme is not an unpleasant place for company in the bathing season, for whose use and accommodation several machines are erected on the beach…. Lyme has a small Assembly Room, Card Room and Billiard table, conveniently arranged under one roof; and had the library been joined to it, all the amusement which the place can furnish would have been comprised in one building. The situation for this edifice is happily chosen, as it commands a charming marine view as far as the Isle of Portland, eight leagues off, and the interior is compact and well arranged.

The Golden Lion and the Three Cups are respectable Inns, and lodgings can generally be procured on easy terms. Lodgings and boarding at Lyme are not merely reasonable, they are even cheap; the dissipations for the healthy, and the suitable accommodation for the sick, are within the reach of ordinary resources. It is frequented principally by persons in the middle class of life…. The resources for intellectual improvement or gratification are here pretty much what they are in places of a similar nature: the libraries are neither copious nor select; although principally composed of novels, many of the best even in that class of books are wanting.

There were certainly two library-cum-bookshops by 1817, Hutchings in Broad Street and Swan's near the Rooms (the family of Swan managed the Assembly Rooms for the Trustees). These are the two booksellers mentioned on the title page of a booklet published locally in 1817, entitled *Picture of Lyme-Regis and Environs*. The author, who admitted he had spent only two days in Lyme, gave his name as M. Phillips; John Fowles wonders whether he might be Molesworth Phillips, who had sailed with Cook – and who was, in fact, brother-in-law to Fanny Burney. By 1817 there was a second indoor baths, in Cobb hamlet, offering hot and cold baths and showers; a church and two dissenting chapels; three "well-conducted Boarding-Schools, two for young Ladies, and one for young Gentlemen"; and three Sunday Schools "happily calculated to instruct the ignorant, and improve the morals of the lower class of people".

Communications were improving: "The arrival of the Post from

The Old Post Office, Coombe Street, showing original posting slot (Author's photo)

London, is about five o'clock in the afternoon, and the western post at noon; the post-office is on Coomb-street; the Mail leaves for London, at nine in the morning".

M. Phillips may have had no lasting interest in the place, but his language recalls the extreme partiality of Mr Parker in *Sanditon*. After using the adjectives "enchanting", "magnificent" and "captivating" of the surrounding scenery, he asserts, "In the spring and autumn, when the frequent variations of the atmosphere operate so unfavorably [*sic*] at most other fashionable resorts for sea bathing; here the fine hills, east, west and north, shelter the Town, which, to use a homely, though a true expression, is a greatcoat warmer than the generality of Watering-places; and in the summer when heat is most oppressive in other parts, the breeze from the Harbour, winding through the outlets, has the effect of a ventilator." It is hard to know quite what he means, and impossible not to suspect that any such breeze from the harbour would be decidedly "fishy", to use Fanny Burney's adjective.

Jane Austen in Lyme; *and Lyme in* **Persuasion**

In 1803, the Austens' tour to the West Country was an autumnal rather than a summer one. Since the sisters seem not to have been apart this year, nothing is in fact known of their summer movements, but by mid-September they were arriving to stay with brother Edward at Godmersham in Kent. Visits to the comfortable and hospitable mansion of Godmersham rarely lasted less than a month, yet it would seem that they had hardly got back to Bath before they were off again, perhaps reluctant to give up the idea of seeing the West Country that year after all. Writing from Southampton five years later, on 7 October 1808, Jane described a fire: "The Flames were considerable, they seemed about as near to us as those at Lyme, & to reach higher. One could not but feel uncomfortable, & I began to think of what I should do, if it came to the worst." [11] This proves that they were in Lyme as late as November 5th, when part of the town round Mill Lane burnt down; it also indicates that they were lodging in the lower reaches of the town, though we cannot be more specific than that.

This November holiday would at least have shown Jane Austen how genial the climate can be even so late in the year, giving her the

JANE AUSTEN'S LYME

(1) Pyne House

(2) Site of the Old Three Cups

(3) Site of the Assembly Rooms

(4) The Walk/Marine Parade

(5) The Jane Austen Garden

(6) "Captain Harville's Cottage"

(7) The Cobb

Benwick & Harville Cottages

THE WALK / MARINE P

(5)

Bathing Ground

Cobb Hamlet

(6)

Monmouth Beach

North Wall

(7)

THE COBB

Gin Shop

Granny's Teeth

Upper Level

Steps

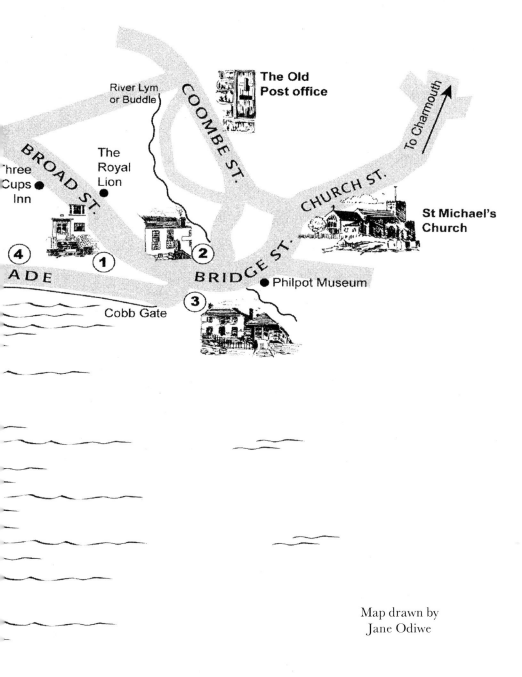

River Lym
or Buddle

**The Old
Post office**

BROAD ST.

The
Royal
Lion

COOMBE ST.

hree
Cups
Inn

CHURCH ST.

To Charmouth

St Michael's
Church

④

①

BRIDGE ST.

②

● Philpot Museum

ADE

③

Cobb Gate

Map drawn by
Jane Odiwe

confidence to set part of *Persuasion* out of doors at Lyme in November 1814 – and even to have her character Mary Musgrove, certainly no stoic, bathe then.

Presumably the 1803 holiday was too short, and too late, for the Austens to feel they had done justice to the charms of the place, as they returned some time in the summer of 1804, in company with Jane's brother Henry and his wife Eliza. Their landlord was a Mr Pyne, and since a property at the bottom of Broad Street belonged to a W. Pyne Esq, this has been accepted as their likely lodging. During one of their rambles, Cassandra made a water-colour sketch of Jane sitting down out of doors, back view, her bonnet strings untied.[12]   It is tantalising not to be able to see her face.

The word "rambles" is Jane Austen's own – or at least, her brother's. The following spring, she wrote to Cassandra of a letter just received from Henry, "He offers to meet us on the Sea-coast …. He talks of the rambles we took together last Summer with pleasing affection."[13]   In about the first week of September, the party divided, Henry, Eliza and Cassandra travelling via Weymouth to friends in Hampshire, the remaining three transferring to cheaper lodgings in Lyme – dirty lodgings, Jane Austen says more in a tone of resignation than disgust. One letter survives from this period of the sisters' separation, and tells us all the little we know of Jane Austen's habits in Lyme.

She danced, she walked, and she bathed, all pretty much as a matter of course. With both her parents she attended the Rooms on both the Wednesday and Thursday evenings preceding her Friday letter to Cassandra. On both evenings her mother played cards: the game of Commerce. How her father occupied himself she does not say (probably reading the newspapers), but "My Father staid very contentedly until half past nine – we went a little after eight - & then walked home with James [a servant] & a Lanthorn, tho' I believe the Lanthorn was not lit, as the Moon was up. But this Lanthorn may sometimes be a great convenience to him."[14]   To warrant this remark to Cassandra suggests the lantern was a novelty, itself suggesting that their new lodgings were further from the Assembly Rooms than their previous lodgings in the lower reaches of Broad Street. Or perhaps the elderly Mr Austen just missed the protection of his son Henry. How the ladies got home, whether James returned for them or they took a sedan chair, is not thought worthy of mention, but "My Mother & I staid about an hour later,

> Nobody asked me the two first dances – the two next I danced with Mr Crawford - & had I chosen to stay longer might have danced with Mr Granville, Mrs Granville's son – whom my dear friend Miss Armstrong offered to introduce to me – or with a new, odd looking Man who had been eyeing me for some time, & at last without any introduction asked me if I meant to dance again. – I think he must be Irish by his ease, & because I imagine him to belong to the Honble Barnwalls, who are the son & son's wife of an Irish Viscount – bold, queerlooking people, just fit to be Quality at Lyme.

On the morning of the ball, which was "pleasant but not full for Thursday," she walked with Miss Armstrong for an hour on the Cobb. The next morning – the morning of the letter – she bathed. "The Bathing was so delightful this morning & Molly so pressing with me to enjoy myself that I believe I staid in rather too long, as since the middle of the day I have felt unreasonably tired. I shall be more careful another time, & shall not bathe tomorrow, as I had before intended." She evidently took full advantage of the opportunities for fresh air and exercise that Lyme afforded. A physical morning and a social evening seems to have been the pattern.

We do not look to Jane Austen's letters for rhapsodising about landscape in the style of Fanny Burney – and of course she had no need to describe or praise Lyme to a sister who had just left. But that the town and its environs made a lasting and favourable impression on her is perfectly clear from the use she made of it, some eleven years later, when she came to write *Persuasion*.

The 'gin shop' steps. Wood-engraving by Joan Hassall,
Folio Society edition of Persuasion, *1975.*

By the time Jane Austen began *Persuasion,* in August 1815, she probably
knew that she would never see the sea again. Her last seaside holiday
as such had been in 1805. Her father had died that January in Bath,
but the three Austen ladies, now living on a much reduced income,
were accompanied to Worthing by brothers Henry and Edward and their
wives. By 1806 they had left Bath and joined households with another
brother, the sailor Francis, in Southampton – actually living by the sea.
In 1809 the three Austen women moved to the cottage on Edward's
Chawton estate, in Jane's beloved Hampshire, where her genius was to
flower in the revision of her first three books and the composition of
her three mature novels, and where she was to feel so evidently
contented and fulfilled. Removed from a city, there was no need for
holidays of escape. Any visits away from Chawton were to the various
brothers and their growing families. Economy and family feeling
determined whatever travel she could manage.

Nevertheless, the sea had held for her special charms. In 1809 it was not impossible she should see the sea again, in company with some kind brother. But by 1815, though she may not quite have begun to feel the symptoms of the disease that was to kill her two years later – those began in 1816 – other family troubles made it unlikely there would ever be any more rambles by the sea. Henry's bank had failed; Edward, though still rich, had also lost money and was widowed with eleven children to raise; James was in ill health and disinclined to leave home; Francis and Charles, the two sailor brothers, could never think in terms of travelling for pleasure (and presumably saw enough of the sea).

Jane Austen's thoughts seemed increasingly to focus on the sea. In the last two novels published in her lifetime, it was the sea itself which had made Portsmouth bearable to Fanny Price in *Mansfield Park*, while the heroine of *Emma* lamented that she had never seen the sea – a deficiency to be remedied on her honeymoon. Now, a passage set in a real seaside place was to form the pivot of her new novel, *Persuasion*, while the fragment that was to remain unfinished at her death, known to us as *Sanditon*, took as its very subject and setting the development of an imaginary seaside resort.

The Lyme scenes in *Persuasion* are beautifully positioned between the long autumnal exposition in the country and the winter denouement of about equal length and weight in Bath. The narrative takes us to Lyme for only one night and the best part of two days: though some of the characters remain there, we and the heroine only hear of them by report. But so much happens in those two days – not only Louisa's dramatic and life-changing accident, but the introduction of two important male characters who are both attracted to Anne, and the dawn of Captain Wentworth's returning love for her – that the two chapters set in Lyme are perhaps the most vivid and memorable in the whole book. It is here in Lyme that the beauties of Anne's character unfold, most importantly in the way she takes control in a crisis, but with lesser intensity in her kindness to Captain Benwick, her openness to new people and places, and her wistful appreciation of the Harvilles' home life. This is Jane Austen writing at the height of her powers, achieving a seamless integration of place, character and action.

But before the characters have taken a step in Lyme, there is a passage of description unique in Jane Austen's fiction – unique in that she seems to indulge herself in personal feeling beyond that which serves the purposes of her novel. The first half of the paragraph could be considered as relating to her characters' perceptions:

> They were come too late in the year for any amusement or variety which Lyme, as a public place, might offer; the rooms were shut up, the lodgers almost all gone, scarcely any family but of the residents left – and, as there is nothing to admire in the buildings themselves, the remarkable situation of the town, the principal street almost hurrying into the water, the walk to the Cobb, skirting round the pleasant little bay, which in the season is animated with bathing machines and company, the Cobb itself, its old wonders and new improvements, with the very beautiful line of cliffs stretching out to the east of the town, are what the stranger's eye will seek;

So far so good; but instead of now taking her characters down to the sea shore and towards the Cobb without more ado, as the action requires, Jane Austen is led into this extraordinary continuation of her musings:

> … and a very strange stranger it must be, who does not see charms in the immediate environs of Lyme, to make him wish to know it better. The scenes in its neighbourhood, Charmouth, with its high grounds and extensive sweeps of country, and still more its sweet retired bay, backed by dark cliffs, where fragments of low rock among the sands make it the happiest spot for watching the flow of the tide, for sitting in unwearied contemplation; - the woody varieties of the cheerful village of Up Lyme, and, above all, Pinny, with its green chasms between romantic rocks, where the scattered forest trees and orchards of luxuriant growth declare that many a generation must have passed away since the first partial falling of the cliff prepared the ground for such a state, where a scene so wonderful and so lovely is exhibited, as

may more than equal any of the resembling scenes of the far-famed Isle of Wight: these places must be visited, and visited again, to make the worth of Lyme understood.

Artistically this is a defect, since the characters have no dealings with Charmouth, Up Lyme or Pinny. For once Jane Austen's rigour has deserted her. Maybe had she lived to see *Persuasion* through the press herself, this passage would have been sacrificed. As it stands, economy and irony, the two most notable characteristics of her prose, are abandoned in favour of guidebook hyperbole. And all, we must feel, out of her exceptional attachment to Lyme. That attachment itself wins us over. Had the seaside interlude in *Persuasion* been set in an imaginary resort, as it perfectly well could have been, we feel it would not have been so powerful in its emotional impact.

The inns, the Walk, the Cobb, the steps, the cottages: these are the specific locations which she makes work for her in *Persuasion*, and we will come back to them in the last chapter. For whereas most places in Jane Austen's novels may be visited only in the imagination, in Lyme, as in Bath, readers have always had the pleasure of walking in the footsteps of her characters.

'A gentleman politely drew back.' Mr Elliot enters the story and Captain Wentworth's admiration of Anne is rekindled in this moment. Illustration by Hugh Thomson for 1897 edition of Persuasion, *republished by Macmillan 1926.*

They came to Lyme
(and thought of Jane)

Many famous people have visited Lyme, from Henry Fielding to Benjamin Disraeli, from Mary Russell Mitford to Beatrix Potter. But a number of writers have either been drawn to Lyme *because* of Jane Austen, or have been reminded of *Persuasion* by their visit.

The most notable of these was Alfred, Lord Tennyson (1809–1892). When looking for a house in 1852 he seriously considered settling in Lyme, although he had never even seen it, purely on account of *Persuasion*.[15] (Instead he bought a house at Farringdon in the Isle of Wight.) Tennyson was a passionate admirer of Jane Austen, comparing her with Shakespeare; as is usual with people who constantly reread her, *Emma* and *Persuasion* were his favourites. In August 1867, at the age of 58, he at last made his pilgrimage to Lyme, walking nine miles from Bridport in company with his friend the poet William Allingham (1824-89). Having refreshed themselves on bread and cheese in Charmouth, the pair took the path over the fields to Lyme, where was living another friend Francis Palgrave (1824-1897), editor of *The Golden Treasury of Rhyme and Song*, on which Tennyson had collaborated. Palgrave recounted the story in a magazine article after Tennyson's death:

Mr Tennyson ... had walked over the hills from Bridport; but no sooner had he entered our Lodgings upon the seawalk than he said, 'Take me now to the Cobb that I may see the steps from which Louisa Musgrove fell', and as I had already, to my own belief, identified these steps, I was at once able to gratify the Poet's curiosity.... The persons she (Miss Austen) created in *Persuasion*, Tennyson remarked as we were returning, were more real and living to him than Monmouth and his followers, whose landing-place on the western side of the Cobb we had just passed.[16]

Poet and novelist Thomas Hardy (1840-1928) and his second wife, Florence, visited Lyme by car on June 10th 1920, a few days after his eightieth birthday. It evidently made him think of Jane Austen, whom he had not read since his youth. It was the Hardys' custom for Florence to read aloud to her husband most evenings; they now plunged into an orgy of Jane Austen, significantly beginning with *Persuasion*. On 8th August that year Florence wrote to Hardy's friend Sydney Cockerell, "We are reading Jane Austen. We have read *Persuasion* and *Northanger Abbey*, and are now in the midst of *Emma*. T.H. is much amused at finding he has *many* characteristics in common with Mr Woodhouse."[17]

The novelist Ivy Compton-Burnett (1894-1969) fled to Lyme from London to escape the V1 and V2 bombs of the Second World War. She was 60 and her companion, Margaret Jourdain, was 70; they remained from January 1944 to April 1945 and evidently felt they were being slightly cowardly. While there, Ivy was asked for a contribution to the first issue of *Orion* and together with Margaret Jourdain produced a question-and-answer piece about the art of writing called 'A Conversation'. I give here the parts relating to Jane Austen:

M.J.: I should like to ask you one or two questions.... There is time enough to spare in Lyme Regis, which is a town well-known to novelists. Jane Austen was here, and Miss Mitford.

I.C-B: And now we are here, though our presence does not seem to be equally felt. No notice marks our lodging. And we also differ from

Jane Austen and Miss Mitford in being birds of passage, fleeing from bombs. I have a feeling that they both would have fled, and felt it proper to do so, and wish that we could really feel it equally proper....

M.J.: Reviewers lean to comparisons. Some have suggested a likeness between your work and Jane Austen's....

I.C-B .... I have read Jane Austen so much, and with such enjoyment and admiration, that I may have absorbed things from her unconsciously....

M.J.: There is little attention given to external things and almost no descriptive writing in your novels, and that is a breach with tradition. Even Jane Austen has an aside about the "worth" of Lyme, Charmouth and Pinhay, "with its green chasms between romantic rocks"....

I.C-B: ... As regards such things as landscape and scenery, I never feel inclined to describe them; indeed I tend to miss such writing out, when I am reading.... In the case of Jane Austen, I hurry through her words about Lyme and its surroundings in order to return to her people.[18]

And then there are the mentions in other people's novels. An early one was *The Trial* (1864) by Charlotte Mary Yonge (1823-1901), whose books Tennyson admired. She had spent a great deal of time in Devon and Dorset with friends in her youth, and knew Lyme well. The heroine of *The Trial*, Ethel May, takes a boating trip to Lyme, and writes to her father, "I could not but think of the Cobb and Louisa Musgrove, as I suppose every one does".

A hundred years later, and in perhaps the second most famous novel of Lyme, *The French Lieutenant's Woman,* an early passage has the hero, Charles Smithson, taking a walk on the Cobb with his fiancée, Ernestina Freeman, who says, "'Now, am I not kind to bring you here? And look." She led him to the side of the rampart, where a line of flat stones inserted sideways into the wall served as rough steps down to a lower walk. "These are the very steps that Jane Austen made Louisa Musgrove fall down in *Persuasion.*'"

Coming right up to our own time we have Inspector Morse …. In *The Way Through the Woods* by Colin Dexter, published in 1992, Chief Superintendent Strange questions Morse about his holiday plans:

"Where are you thinking of?"

"Lyme Regis."

"Ah. Glorious Devon."

"Dorset, sir."

"Next door, surely?"

"*Persuasion* – it's where some of the scenes in *Persuasion* are set."

"Ah." Strange looked suitably blank.

"And *The French Lieutenant's Woman.*"

Jane Austen's Lyme Today

Sites with Jane Austen connections are discussed here in the order they would be encountered by a walker, and are numbered to correspond with the map on pp 26-27. The trail begins in the heart of the town at the foot of Broad Street.

1. Pyne House

In all probability, Jane Austen stayed in three different lodgings in Lyme, but this is the only one of which we can be reasonably confident.

The Austens' first lodgings in Lyme, in the autumn of 1803, are unknown. The only clue is that they were near to the fire which broke out at Crossman's, a baker, in Mill Lane on November 5th, consuming 42 houses. This implies only that the Austens were in the town itself, as we would expect, rather than in the Cobb hamlet, or on the hill.

On arrival in the summer of 1804, having joined forces with Henry and Eliza, they needed – and could afford – more space. This is when they probably rented the property known as Pyne House, near the bottom of Broad Street on the South side. (Broad Street actually runs West to East, not North to South as is often supposed.) This informed guess is based on the fact that in her one surviving letter from Lyme, Jane Austen mentions having written to Mr Pyne, in terms that suggest

Pyne House, 10 Broad Street. The plaque was erected by the Town Council in 1984 and reads: This is the most likely lodging of Jane Austen, whose visits to Lyme in 1803 and 1804 gave birth to her novel Persuasion. *(Author's photo)*

he was the landlord, about a broken lid. A plan of 1824 clearly shows a property labelled 'W Pyne Esq' in this location.

The house is shown in a watercolour of about the 1820s with a thronging cattle and general market, known as the Shambles, pressing up against its front door. Until the 1840s, the lower reaches of Broad Street contained a terrace of three buildings in the middle of the street, known appropriately as Middle Row, while extending beyond them, as the map of 1824 clearly shows, were the market structures, passing in front of Pyne House. The street scene then, would have been a cramped, noisy and smelly one, though agreeably near the sea. Certainly Jane Austen's remark that the furniture altogether was scarcely worth five shillings, though an amusing exaggeration, suggests that these were not very genteel lodgings. But at this date, genteel lodgings were hardly to be got in Lyme.

By the time Jane was informing Cassandra of her letter to Mr Pyne,

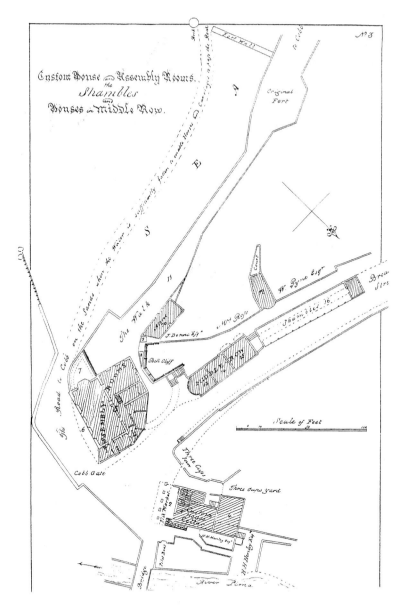

1824 town plan showing lower part of Broad Street. Clearly marked are the Assembly Rooms, the original Three Cups Inn and its stable yard, and the house belonging to Wm Pyne Esq., where the Austens are thought to have lodged in 1804. The Shambles (open market) is right outside the front door.

(Courtesy of the Philpot Museum, Lyme Regis)

the family had already moved to different lodgings. Presumably on the division of the party smaller and more economical lodgings were required by the remaining three. Of their new quarters Jane writes, "Nothing certainly can exceed the inconvenience of the offices, except the general dirtiness of the house & furniture & all its inhabitants ... I detect dirt in the water-decanter as fast as I can". There is no clue to the location of these inferior lodgings, but we can guess that they must have been further away than Pyne House from the Assembly Rooms as there was a new arrangement, which Jane felt worth remarking to Cassandra, of walking home at night with a manservant and lantern. It is very unlikely that, with their fondness for attending the Rooms at night, they would have chosen to lodge in Cobb hamlet, requiring a longish walk in the dark along the shore or cliffs - as we shall see, the path was very uncertain - much more likely that the new lodgings were in one of the unlit, possibly unsavoury, narrow streets of the old town.

That the Austens chose to return for a second year to Lyme, and that after Henry, Eliza and Cassandra had left the others stayed in the town rather than move on themselves, is a tribute to how little the quality of their lodgings mattered to them in comparison with the beauty of the landscape and pleasures of the place itself.

2. The two inns

There has been much argument about which of "the two inns" mentioned in *Persuasion* the Musgrove party were occupying when they watched Mr Elliot's curricle up the hill.

In the early nineteenth century, the two principal inns were the Three Cups and the Lion, of which the former was the more fashionable. That alone might make it the natural choice of Mr Elliot and the Musgroves. The 1817 *Picture of Lyme-Regis* mentions the Three Cups, kept by Mr Manning, as "An excellent house where all are accommodated in every way agreeable to the wish of the visitant" but does not mention the Lion. (There was also the George, in George's Square, but that was used chiefly by traders.) The Three Cups (which took its name from the arms of the Salters' Company – extracting salt from the sea was once a major industry in Lyme) was the very last building at the bottom of Broad Street on the North side; it can be quite clearly seen on Drayton's 1824 plan, and in a print of about 1840. Also marked is the Three Cups Yard, round the corner, which agrees with the description in *Persuasion*, of Mr Elliot's curricle "coming round from the stable-yard to the front door". The Lion, however, did not then front Broad Street, as it was set back behind a court, a little way up from the Three Cups on the same side; no view up the hill would have been possible from its windows.

What makes things extremely confusing for modern visitors is that, while we can usually rely on old inns to remain where they have always stood, that is not the case in Lyme. The Lion, having been renamed The Royal Lion after a visit from the future Edward VII in the middle of the nineteenth century, was extended forwards to front Broad Street, and now has large square bay windows, ideal for looking up the hill. Meanwhile the Three Cups burnt down in 1844 and was rebuilt on the other side of the street, a little way up, with its own private walkway past the back of Pyne House and other buildings down to Marine Parade. The new Three Cups also has prominent bay windows, in this case rounded ones.

Though this building very clearly still bears the name of the Three Cups, it has been kept empty and unused by the brewery that owns it since 1991. It is a pity that such an ancient name from Lyme's history should have fallen into disuse, and even more poignant since it was in this building that local people met in 1930 to form the Lyme Regis Society, with the objective of saving historic buildings.

So, sadly, while there are very obviously two major old inns with bay windows at either one of which we might imagine the clustered Musgrove party looking out, our imagination would be unjustified by the facts. The window from which they looked has now gone. However, the cellars of the old Three Cups remain, and can be visited as part of the Sanctuary Bookshop, 65 Broad Street.

(For those who cannot get to Lyme Regis but who have access to the video of *The French Lieutenant's Woman*, the [new] Three Cups can be seen in the Victorian scenes as the quarters of Charles Smithson [Jeremy Irons]; later Irons and Meryl Streep, playing the present-day actors making the film, can be seen issuing from the Royal Lion. The film also gives a good view of Broad Street generally, altered to look like the 1860s, complete with market.)

3. Site of the Assembly Rooms
Also marked on the 1824 plan. Alas, the Assembly Rooms have long gone, demolished to make way for a car park. In one of the digressions into modern times that are characteristic of *The French Lieutenant's Woman*, John Fowles writes:

> The Lyme Assembly Rooms were perhaps not much, compared to those at Bath and Cheltenham; but they were pleasing, with their spacious proportions and windows facing the sea. Too pleasing, alas, and too excellent a common meeting-place not to be sacrificed to that Great British God, Convenience; and they were accordingly long ago pulled down....

It has very wittily been remarked that this site, at the very pivot of Lyme where Broad Street tumbles into the sea, epitomises the three successive sources of its prosperity – trade, fashion, and mass tourism. The area is called Cobb Gate, and there was once a real gate here, through which all imported goods, having been pulled by horses across the sands, had to pass on their way to the Customs House nearby. The site was occupied by warehouses, which were no longer required when trade diminished in the eighteenth century. As we have seen, as part of his plan to promote Lyme as a resort, Thomas Hollis purchased the old warehouses to make way for Assembly Rooms in the mid-1770s. For perhaps three-quarters of a century, they were the focus of fashionable life in Lyme, but with a change in social habits, became less and less frequented. Just before the First World War they were privately purchased and converted to a cinema and tea-shop, but that did not last long, and after they had been damaged in a storm of 1927, they were pulled down. Perhaps it was this outrage which prompted some citizens to get together three years later to form the Lyme Regis Society, mentioned above.

There never seems to have been any plan to redevelop the site for anything but a car park – and conveniences. Great and genuine though the need is for parking in any thriving town, it does seem a shame to have cars in such a very visible spot.

Fortunately for us, when Constance Hill came on her Austen pilgrimage in 1901 – exactly midway between Jane Austen's time and our own – the Rooms were still there for her to visit. In her book *Jane Austen, her Homes and her Friends* she has left a charming description, worth reading as we stand on the spot:

> The ball-room is little changed since Miss Austen danced in it that September evening nearly a hundred years ago. It has lost its three glass chandeliers which used to hang from the arched ceiling, but these may still be seen in a private house in the neighbourhood…. We visited the room by daylight, and felt almost as if it were afloat, for nothing but blue sea and sky was to be seen from its many windows. From the wide recessed window at the end, however, we got a glimpse of the sands and of the harbour and Cobb beyond.

Incidentally, something of this feeling of being afloat in a building may be experienced today in two nearby premises open to the public, the Philpot Museum and the Marine Theatre (which may some time in the future be renamed the Jane Austen Theatre in tribute to the town's most illustrious visitor, though there was not a theatre here at that time). Old pictures show how the Assembly Rooms perched at the water's edge. It seems astonishing to build them so close (was Thomas Hollis playing on the eighteenth-century mania for being genteelly frightened?) and of course, it *was* the sea that finally undermined them.

View of lower Broad Street, c. 1844. The word 'hotel' can be seen on the old Three Cups. The rooftops on the far right belong to the Assembly Rooms.

An oil painting by Read of 1815, depicting a storm dashing the sea against the Rooms, has been reproduced in colour on the cover of a recent Penguin edition (and audiobook) of *Persuasion*.

The steps up from the beach where Mr Elliot "politely drew back" and first admired his cousin Anne, were most probably the substantial flight just below the Assembly Rooms, now gone. It is these steps that the party from Uppercross descend on their first exploration of the town.

4. The Walk / Marine Parade

Though Jane Austen does not dignify it with a capital letter, she does mention "the walk to the Cobb, skirting round the pleasant little bay" (and maybe she did use the capital – the printer of this posthumously published novel may well be guilty of altering her intention). At the time of *Persuasion* known as the Walk, subsequently as Marine Parade, this is the footway which she herself used when she went bathing, and a later version of which her characters traverse on the two occasions when they walk from their inn to the Cobb. We can also imagine Captain Benwick "flying" along here in quest of a surgeon in the town.

We know that Thomas Hollis had been the first to appreciate the necessity of a Walk – that is a promenade for genteel visitors, as opposed to a utilitarian footpath – along the shore at Lyme. But such is both the power of the sea and the instability of the land in this area, that nature kept thwarting man's intent.

A plan of 1796 shows "a summer footpath to town" along the shore between the Cobb and Cobb Gate, only Alcove Cottage, the very first property after the Assembly Rooms, then existing. "The Alcove" had been a glazed-in recess where the very earliest visitors to Lyme danced before the Assembly Rooms were built. Subsequently the site reverted to storage space for boats and coals, before a cottage was built on the spot.

This summer footpath, or a walk across the sands at low tide, was all that linked the two parts of Lyme at the time of Jane Austen's visits. In 1809 a Court Leet Jury declared the path dangerous, and an attempt was made to level a new one, but this was soon washed away by the sea. A more ambitious effort was made in 1811, when £2,500 was raised by subscription to construct a walk with a small retaining wall. The Guide Book of 1811 says "The principal walk at Lyme Regis has been much improved, being now completely separated from the sea by a new breakwater". This was wishful thinking, and a map of 1813 shows "New Wall and Walk partly destroyed by the Tides". Another effort was made. The 1817 *Picture of Lyme-Regis* talks of "a new walk *nearly* completed, between the Town and Harbour, along the Clifts; which, from its elevated situation, commands a fine view" [my italics]. Jane Austen had therefore not seen the precise state of the Walk that she made her characters pass along in November 1814.

The 1824 map makes it clear that there was still no property beyond Alcove Cottage until one reached the remains of an old fort, halfway along. On this map the Walk is still so named, and also drawn in is "The Road to Cobb on the Sands when the Water is sufficiently fallen to enable Horses and Carriages to pass the Rock". Some time after 1826 the name was changed to Marine Parade, though the old name lingered in the townsfolk's affections, and thereafter houses began to be built along it from the town towards the Cobb. The instability of the land stopped them halfway, and even now the Council has problems propping up the land.

Of the houses one can see today in Marine Parade, a particularly attractive row of four, pink-washed, bow-windowed and thatched, includes cottages named for Captains Harville and Benwick. This is a charming tribute to *Persuasion,* but though they have a Regency air, the cottages post-date the novel (c.1830). Francis Palgrave, in the mid-nineteenth century, was the first to make the claim that this was where the Harvilles lodged, but the claim must be erroneous. Even in her imagination Jane Austen is unlikely to have placed the Harvilles on this spot, since she could not have surmised that dwellings would ever be built here – and anyway, the Harville residence is not meant to be fashionable and new.

5. *The Jane Austen Garden*
Towards the Cobb end of Marine Parade, just before Cobb Lane begins, is to be found a little steeply terraced garden dedicated to Jane Austen.

From the beginning of the twentieth century, a myth grew up that Jane Austen had lodged in a house on this site. As myths do, it took hold and was repeated in books about both Lyme Regis and Jane Austen. The myth has even been embellished so that some townsfolk will tell you that "part of *Persuasion* was written here" – whereas, of course, *Persuasion* was not begun until 1815.

The house in question was called Wings and was built into the hillside, on odd levels, with low ceilings and a narrow, twisting staircase – but delightful views. Constance Hill set the myth going in print when she visited Lyme in 1901 and was told by some locals that Wings had been the Austen lodging – this word-of-mouth she describes as "good authority". The Lyme historian Cyril Wanklyn, writing in 1927, says "the house occupied by the family can still be seen at the west end of the Walk, though why it is called 'Wings' no man knows. It still has 'two ground floors' (a characteristic of many Lyme Regis houses built on sloping ground) and has probably not changed much since Jane Austen's day".[28] However, prints and maps show that Wings was not even built in 1804 – or for many years after. Though a specific building date is not recorded, it seems to have been part of the expansion of Lyme along the water's edge, wherever a foothold could be hazarded, of the 1830s and 40s.

In 1945 the house fell victim to landslip, and was demolished. Thirty years later, to commemorate the bicentenary of her birth, the Jane Austen Society, in conjunction with Lyme Regis Town Council, established a garden memorial here.

The original plaque having become largely illegible, a second plaque was erected by the Society to mark the millennium – for despite the dubious claims of the site, all lovers of Jane Austen's novels must delight in having a corner of this charming town dedicated to the author whom it so happily inspired.

The bust which also adorns the garden is something of a mystery. It cannot, of course, be Jane Austen – no bust was made of her in her lifetime – but it gives a pleasantly feminine touch to the garden, and does no harm. It is believed to be the work of one Percy Fitzgerald, around 1917, and to have formerly been on display in Bath, but its provenance – and even more, how it came to Lyme - has proved difficult to establish. Perhaps more information will come to light in the future.

The bust by Percy Fitzgerald in the Jane Austen Garden (Author's photo)

6. *"Captain Harville's Cottage"*

The first thing to be said in connection with the Harvilles' home in *Persuasion* is that this is self-evidently a fictional construct. Jane Austen would not have had any specific building in mind any more than she based Kellynch or Uppercross on real houses. It would have seemed impertinent to her to purloin any real person's home for her fiction. Writing *Persuasion* eleven years after her last visit to Lyme, she would have had no more than a general location in mind.

That location, according to clues in the text, has to be on the townward side of the Cobb – and almost certainly nearer to the Cobb than the town. The only specific is "at the foot of a pier of unknown date" – an odd detail, since one wouldn't expect to know the date of a pier unless one were an historian. But nothing that could be called a pier has ever been shown on a map of Lyme. Other than short breakwaters and jetties, the only marine structure apart from the Cobb is the detached outer wall that runs almost parallel to it, and is marked on the 1796 map as "old wall much out of repair".

The landward end of this wall is close to the cluster of buildings on the seaward side of Cobb Lane (as the Walk becomes at this point). Properties here are marked as "Mr Coade's" on the 1796 map and as "Coade's first buildings on the beach" in 1813. This corner of (mainly) dry land had been reclaimed from the sea after the gap between the Cobb and the land had been closed in 1756, allowing the angle between them to silt up. The Coades were one of the two major landowning families of Lyme.

This is where it has been traditional to imagine Captain Harville's cottage, and the supposition is entirely reasonable. Constance Hill was quite convinced that it was Bay Cottage - so were its then owners, and the identification continues to serve, since part of Bay Cottage is now "Jane's Takeaway". A building in this spot would fit the story, though we need not suppose that Jane Austen had any particular cottage in view, or that, given the great storm of 1824 and the many storms that have buffeted Lyme thereafter, the present buildings are exactly as they would have been in 1804, 1815 or even 1901.

7. The steps where Louisa Musgrove fell

The Cobb was breached in storms of both January 1817 and November 1824, and was substantially rebuilt in 1825, as a very full plaque halfway along the wall recounts. So we cannot say that the Cobb is stone-for-stone as Jane Austen and the Musgroves would have known it.

As it stands, there are three sets of steps to choose from. The first (in order as you walk along the Cobb) is the double flight on either side of what is known locally as "the gin shop" – gin being a word for a crane or hoist. Here ammunition was once kept. In this alcove the 1825 plaque is situated, and although there was certainly a place marked "gin shop" on the map of 1813, the evenness of the steps, and the placing of the plaque, suggests that this set of steps dates from the rebuilding. It is, however, the set chosen by Joan Hassall for her wood engraving illustrating Louisa's fall in the Folio edition of *Persuasion,* and for the 1971 BBC TV adaptation.

Granny's Teeth, The Cobb

Next we come to "Granny's teeth", traditional name for blocks of stone projecting unsupported from the wall: the most terrifying of the three possibilities. Even in jeans and trainers one cannot imagine "running" up these steps, let alone in long skirts. However, these are certainly the steps most frequently identified with Louisa's accident, and the character of the stonework, as well as of the steps themselves, suggests they do belong to the oldest surviving part of the Cobb, when life and limb were held cheap. John Fowles, in the passage already quoted from *The French Lieutenant's Woman*, endorses these as the all-important steps; and these were the ones chosen for the 1995 film of *Persuasion*.

The final set of steps is the most ordinary in design, though still without a handrail and therefore capable of causing an accident. The argument against identifying these with the passage in *Persuasion* is that they are almost at the far end of the Cobb. If the wind was too great for the ladies to walk along the upper level in comfort, they would hardly have proceeded so far before they descended.

Even without the wind, the steeply cambered surface of the present Upper Cobb, sloping towards the sheer drop to the open sea, would make it an unsafe place for ladies in long dresses to walk very far, one would have thought. But neither steps, nor stones, nor surfaces, are exactly as they were in 1815 – or in Jane Austen's memory and imagination.

The novelist and local historian John Fowles, whose knowledge of Lyme and the Cobb is unsurpassed, goes so far as to suggest that it was impossible to promenade on the Upper Walk before 1817; in this he follows George Roberts, who in 1834 wrote that "the parapet from the gin shop to the outer pier was too rough for a promenade" before the improvements made after the 1817 storm. Yet this "impossibility" is exactly what Jane Austen has her characters do. It is a salutary reminder, as we seek to peg our favourite novels to reality, that we must not be too literal about the imaginative process.

Returning to the town, there are a few more places to see to complete our experience of Jane Austen's Lyme. As we walk back, we pass the "Bathing Ground" (8) where the four bathing machines were located in 1804, at the Cobb hamlet end of the main beach. In the town, the Philpot Museum (9) tells Lyme's history, including its many literary associations, and has a display of Austen artefacts generously lent by Lyme Regis resident Mrs Diana Shervington, who is doubly descended from Jane Austen's brother Edward. In Coombe Street (10) may be seen the old Post Office, in use from 1799 to 1853, complete with its original posting slot. This, presumably, is where Jane Austen posted the letter to Cassandra dated 14 September 1804 – an action which in its ordinariness seems to bring her very close to us. Finally there is St Michael's Church (11) where she and her family would have worshipped. From this side of town the energetic can walk over the cliffs to Charmouth, as Jane Austen loved to do. The less energetic, of course, can still extend their pilgrimage by driving to Charmouth to watch "the flow of the tide" and to sit "in unwearied contemplation" of this lovely stretch of coast.

Charmouth Dorset from Catherstone

Bibliography

— *Lyme Regis Walkabout*, Serendip Fine Books, 2002

— *Signs of History*, The Lyme Regis Society, 2002

Austen, Jane, *Persuasion*, Clarendon Edition edited by R.W. Chapman, Oxford University Press, revised edition, 1965

Austen-Leigh, R.A., *Jane Austen and Lyme Regis*, Spottiswoode, Ballantyne & Co. Ltd., 1941

Fowles, John, *A Short History of Lyme Regis*, The Dovecote Press, 1991

Fowles, John, *The French Lieutenant's Woman*, Jonathan Cape, 1969

Hill, Constance, *Jane Austen, Her Homes and Her Friends*, The Bodley Head, 1901 and 1923

Lane, Maggie, *Jane Austen's England*, Robert Hale, 1986

Lane, Maggie, *Jane Austen's World*, Carlton Books, 1996

Le Faye, Deirdre, *Jane Austen: A Family Record*, The British Library, 1989

Le Faye, Deirdre (editor), *Jane Austen's Letters*, Oxford University Press, 1995

Lello, John, *Lyme Regis Past*, Lello Publishing, 1999

Roberts, George, *History of Lyme Regis*, 1834

Wanklyn, Cyril, *Lyme Regis, A Retrospect*, 1927

Notes

1. *Letters*, p.68
2. *Letters*, p.56
3. *Letters, p.*71
4. Le Faye, Deirdre, *Jane Austen's Outlandish Cousin*, British Library 2002, p.160
5. *Letters*, p.71
6. Fowles, John, *A Short History of Lyme Regis*, The Dovecote Press, 1991, p.7 This is the chief source of most of the historical facts about Lyme which follow.
7. Draper, Jo, *The Georgians (Discover Dorset)*, The Dovecote Press, 1998, p.22
8. Le Faye, 2002, *op. cit.*, p.99
9. Hemlow, Joyce (editor), *Fanny Burney Journals and Letters, Volume I*, Oxford University Press, 1972, p.26
10. Hemlow, *op. cit.*, p.25
11. *Letters*, p.144

12. The picture is signed 'C.E.A. 1804' and is described by Anna Lefroy, Jane Austen's niece, as "a sketch which Aunt Cassandra made of her in one of their expeditions" which had "a good deal of resemblance" in the figure: Lefroy Manuscript, private possession, quoted in Le Faye, 1989.
13. *Letters*, p.102
14. *Letters, p.95*
15. Levi, Peter, *Tennyson*, Macmillan 1993, p.267
16. Palgrave, Francis, 'Miss Austen at Lyme' in *The Grove*, 1891, p.59. Quoted in Austen-Leigh, Emma, *Jane Austen and Lyme Regis*, Spottiswoode, Ballantyne, 1940, p.56. William Allingham's *Journal* for August 23 1867 describes the walk, bread and cheese, etc; edited by John Grigson, it was published in 1967. Quoted in Levi, *op.cit.*
17. Meynell, Viola (editor), *Friends of a Lifetime: Letters to Sydney Carlyle Cockerell*, p.306, quoted in Millgate, Michael, *Thomas Hardy*, Oxford University Press, 1982, p.531
18. Sprigge, Elizabeth, *The Life of Ivy Compton-Burnett*, Gollancz, 1973, p.110